John,

Lead Well!

Rick Lochner

# The Missing Piece

By Richard A. Lochner Jr.

ISBN-13: 978-0615670553
RPC Books
www.MissingPieceBook.com

A Branded Imprint of

RPC Books
rpcleadershipassociates.com

# ACKNOWLEDGEMENTS

Successful business books, like successful leaders, do not happen by chance. I am truly humbled by the level of support for this project beginning with Paul and Nora Kardian, whose early support of RPC Leadership Associates, Inc. created a platform to bring this idea to reality. To the many employees whom I have had the honor to lead who executed and helped refine the model to its present incarnation. To the numerous clients who embraced The Model and realized its value to their organizations. They are the real reason this book was written.

Many thanks to those who provided their candid insights into the best method to effectively communicate The Model's value including Greg Stuart, Susan Nielsen, Robyn Rickenbach and Tammy Kohl. A very special Thank You to Jim Godshall for so freely sharing his wisdom on how best to leverage The Model through this book.

I could not have asked for a better group of expertise to help make this book a reality. Each took on a piece of the project as if it were their personal project. The editing by Elizabeth Kane and Danielle Willis proved invaluable to create a great finished product. The graphics from Paul Feith at Paul Gregory Media helped bring The Model to life from cover to cover. Julia Newton at Archer Graphic Design created the layout to optimize the overall experience for the reader. Sarah Bruns at inGauge, Inc. was instrumental in creating the final title and craft the story behind the book. Many thanks to Don and Kate Gingold who willingly shared their own publishing experiences to help wade through the many choices.

And finally, I cannot thank my family enough for their unconditional support, patience and insight to bring this book to reality. Everyone helped in some way to bring it all together and you were truly an inspiration to me throughout the entire process.

**Thank You!**

## DEDICATION

*To Colleen whose love and support inspires me daily and to Rich, Paul, Chris and Laurel who are my constant reminder why we make leadership a way of life for their future!*

# TABLE OF CONTENTS

# FOREWORD

# Foreword

Every once in a while a business book is written that is indeed a road map to becoming a business success. *The Missing Piece* is one of those books. Rick has developed a model that not only sheds light on the various aspects of business, but he does so in a simplified and logical manner that is easy to read, understand and implement.

Part of the book's beauty is after explaining a principal and how it fits, the reader is given an opportunity to do a self-assessment. As the reader progresses through the various aspects of the **"Business Alignment Maturity Model© (BAMM)"** they will end up with an understanding of where they can improve their own business.

The overriding principle is seeing the interrelationships of the various pieces which are critical to produce a smoothly functioning business. It clearly points out that improvement can only come from looking at how the pieces align with each other. Lacking an understanding of this alignment principal perhaps explains why quick fixes don't work.

In the past, we have observed that if management doesn't know why they aren't achieving results, they "play" leader. Often they reason that any activity is better than doing nothing so they move individual pieces of the business without regard to causes and effects. Popular meddling activities we have seen are things such as:

- Restructuring without regard as to why, or

- Announcing a different compensation program without regard as to how it fits with strategy, or starting "programs-de-jour" because others are doing them, or

- Developing a strategic plan without implementation plans, or prodding people with slogans, or setting goals without input from those who must achieve them, or

- Promoting people just to get a new face but who have not been properly developed, or

- Explaining desired results without focus on the customer.

These are but a few we have seen and rarely have the results been positive or lasting. In fact, conditions often get worse.

This random meddling or pseudo-leadership results from not seeing or understanding how everything works together. After reading this book and understanding BAMM, the game of business becomes clear.

Understanding produces enlightenment. Enlightenment produces improved results. Improved results produces leadership because no one wants to follow a loser. The BAMM model can help business leaders achieve conscious success. Well worth the read.


James Godshall
President, Total Quality Institute

(Mr. Godshall is an internationally recognized business leader, consultant and author of continuous quality improvement materials used throughout the world)

# INTRODUCTION

# Introduction

What does double-digit growth look like for your business? How would a 20% increase in customer satisfaction impact your business? What about a double-digit increase in Gross Margin? There are literally tens of thousands of business books, magazines and articles written outlining how large organizations achieve these types of results. Many are research based and provide a wealth of information. So why would I write another one and how is this one any different?

I did not just write a book, I am telling a story. Actually, I am telling several stories around a single central idea. These are stories that readers who are Entrepreneurs, Corporate Leaders, Non-Profit Board Members/ Leaders or individual Professionals will relate to because they are based on real people, real organizations and real events. The characterizations represented here are composites of people and businesses I have had the privilege of working for or working with over the last thirty years.

Many of the business books I read hold up the usual large, successful companies like Southwest Airlines as examples of how to best run a successful business. I am a loyal Southwest flier, but I struggle with connecting their history and success to the growing manufacturing company expanding to new global markets, or the non-profit looking to reengineer its fundraising strategy or the entrepreneur trying to grow his/her fledgling business. Many of the business books I read are also centered on a single topic or piece of research, which is a great way to become further educated on one specific topic. Unfortunately, it is never one thing that creates success for businesses in today's global economy. It is through aligning the multiple moving parts of the business where Visions are realized, where Strategies are fulfilled and Goals achieve Desired Results.

I wrote this book because I see too many organizations talking around or speaking to business alignment in vague terms. It is a topic that in a dynamic business, political and economic environment, it is difficult to execute because it involves multiple moving parts working together in unison to achieve success. It also takes time to do well so it often gets lost in the misplaced efforts to achieve instant, but fleeting, success. In essence, this is a book about the leadership required to achieve business alignment because it is through effective leadership that sustainable business success occurs. Leaders today must embrace the idea of Realistic Performance Change to achieve sustainable success.

Why Business Alignment? We define business alignment as the process of matching the organization's tactics to the available or readily acquirable resources to achieve its strategic objectives. While defined in a rather straightforward manner, its execution is far from straightforward.

Have you ever tried to build a 500-piece jigsaw puzzle without looking at the picture on the cover of the box? It can be done, but it would be a slow, frustrating process. The picture on the puzzle box is what success looks like; the completed puzzle. I do not know many people who would consciously attempt such a thing. Yet, I find business owners and organizational leaders doing exactly that, running businesses without having a clear picture of success outlined and visible for all stakeholders.

The Business Alignment Maturity Model© (BAMM) is the picture on the box. It provides a blueprint for combining every part (or piece) of a business to achieve the picture of success. It also determines what parts of the business are working for or against the strategic direction of the business. As a business follows the multiple stages of alignment in this approach, the more aligned it becomes across the full breadth of its capabilities, and the better it achieves its desired results. This book explains how to make the **Business Alignment Maturity Model© (BAMM)** (henceforth referred to as The Model) work for your business or non-profit.

# PROLOGUE

# *Prologue*

The book is organized in *three* distinct sections. **Section 1** speaks to Strategic Thinking, or the part of the alignment process outlining the direction and purpose of the organization. It speaks to how organizational leaders think through the Vision of the organization and the framework for how the organization competes in its industry and markets to achieve the first two Stages of Business Alignment. **Section 2** outlines the key Operational Support Elements necessary to successfully bridge the Strategic Thinking process and effective Tactical Execution. **Section 3** speaks directly to the Tactical Execution and how aligned goals and control systems lead to achieving desired organizational results and advance to complete Business Alignment.

My purpose in writing this book is to tell how three representative organizational leaders leveraged the power of business alignment to achieve their desired results. These characters are composites of the many leaders I have worked with over the years, not real individuals. Our stories begin:

- *Carlos* is the Chief Executive Officer for a manufacturer of molded plastic components. They operate in four countries and are in a good position to grow over 40% in the next three years. Most of their business (over 80%) had come from domestic operations leading up to the most recent downturn in the economy. They are poised to expand existing international operations as well as establish new operations in developing international markets beyond their current presence. The leadership team is focused on scaling their leadership capabilities and operational processes to effectively grow the business while staying true to their Vision.

- *Chrissy* is very active on the board of directors for a non-profit that helps at-risk teens develop life skills to prepare them for life after high school. They receive 55% of their funding from state grants, a troublesome situation given the current status of the state's budget deficit. She is a high school English teacher and has never worked in the business world. However, she has a very good relationship with the Executive Director, who, after several years in the position, is now poised to take the organization to new levels of program support. The organization has a very rudimentary business plan and little expertise on the board to help with strategic planning. However, the board must find new sources of revenue if the non-profit is to survive.

- *Phil* is an entrepreneur who owns a retail store selling fitness gear targeted to the Baby Boomers. A fitness aficionado, he sees a growing need for fitness gear targeted to the growing senior population. His four-year old business held its own during the recent downturn in the economy turning a very minimal profit. However, he must revisit his business model as he does not yet have an online presence and is concerned with the declining foot traffic into his store.

# OVERVIEW OF THE MODEL

As *Carlos, Chrissy* and *Phil* apply The Model to their respective businesses throughout the book, their journey will take them through each of the layers on the graphic below.

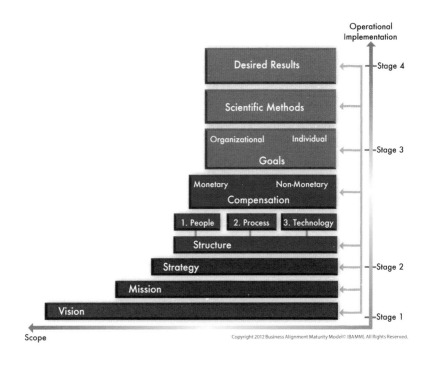

The Horizontal Axis denotes the scope of each layer in The Model in terms of timeframe. The lower layers of The Model have a much broader time scope than the higher layers. While the diagram is not drawn to exact scale by design, it does reflect the relative differences in the time scope of each layer as we work up through The Model.

The Vertical Axis denotes the Stage of operational implementation by the organization as it navigates the alignment process. Secondarily, the height of each layer denotes a level of relative complexity in creating and maintaining alignment, especially at the higher layers.

This combination creates an exponential curve in The Model from Stage 1 through Stage 4 Business Alignment.

Finally, it should be noted that each layer of The Model must be aligned with the layer below it before moving to the next layer in the process. For example, when the organization creates the Mission Statement they must actively reconcile the Mission to the existing or previously completed vision Statement before moving on to create the Strategy. In day-to-day language, the alignment messaging could sound something like, "Our Mission is … to help us achieve our overall Vision of …" When stakeholders hear the message and understand it, the organization can effectively move forward through the alignment process. This process of reconciling layers is repeated through all eight layers of The Model. Achieving Stage 5 Business Alignment and sustainable business success depends on the foundational alignment in business operations.

I have yet to work for or work with an organization that could not leverage The Model to achieve greater success. Each of the characterizations above are used throughout the book to represent the leaders and organizations large and small, for-profit and not-for-profit, who can leverage the value of The Model to achieve desired results. The level of effort varies with the scope and scale of the business, but the underlying concept is the same.

While certain key points may be made using one of the three characterizations, the points apply to all three albeit in different ways.

So let's take a journey with *Carlos, Chrissy* and *Phil* as they leverage the **Business Alignment Maturity Model© (BAMM)** to achieve success in their respective businesses.

*Starting To Put The Missing Pieces Together...*

## Section 1 Puzzle Piece

### 1. Strategic Thinking

## 2. Operational Support Elements

## 3. Tactical Execution

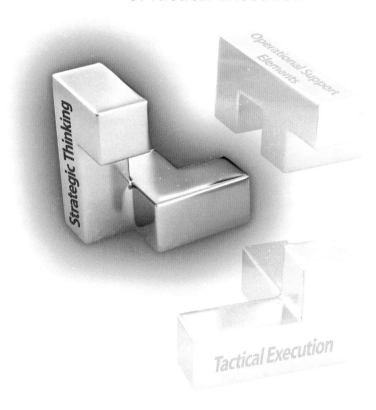

# SECTION 1 ~
# Strategic Thinking:

# *Section I: Strategic Thinking*

This section introduces the first two Stages of business alignment in The Model through the Strategic Thinking process. Stage 1 alignment is achieved through the creation of an organizational Vision. However, simply creating a Vision is not enough to create the level of alignment required for sustainable success. Stage 2 alignment is achieved through the creation of a business Strategy which, when executed, creates the desired future outlined in the Vision. The Strategic Thinking process is creating:

- A Vision of a desired future

- A Mission to break the desired future into tangible and meaningful direction

- A Strategy identifying how the organization will compete

Creating an organizational Vision, Mission and Strategy collectively forms the foundation for effective business alignment for any type of organization, of any size and in any industry. When all else fails, the outcome of the Strategic Thinking process helps an organization manage change, adapt to shifts in their internal environment and clearly identify how they will compete to achieve their desired results.

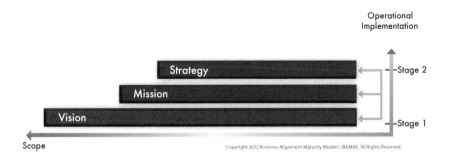

# CHAPTER 1:

## "I can see clearly now..."

*~ it all begins with a clear Vision*

**THE KEY POINT:** Success begins with a Purpose. An organization's Purpose is typically defined through the combination of Vision and Mission statements. In many cases, the Values of an organization or business may be explicitly stated as opposed to implied through the Vision and Mission. Regardless, successfully aligning all elements of any business, for-profit or non-profit, begins with a Vision of a future to aspire to. If your organization has a Vision, is it still the right Vision for the next three to five years? While Mission Statements (Chapter 2) are valuable, they are not a replacement for a well-crafted Vision Statement. And not having a Vision as a business, large or small, is a recipe for inefficiency due to loss of directional focus.

The first Stage of alignment in The Model is creating and sharing a Vision for the organization. A Vision is a short statement declaring what the organization aspires to become and achieve at some point in the future, usually three to five years out. For instance, the Vision of my current company, RPC Leadership Associates, Inc. is "Making Leadership a Way of Life." The Vision answers the question "What is the desired future state of your organization and what do its leaders collectively aspire to in the next five years?" It paints a picture of a desired future, one that stakeholders can embrace and leverage as a focal point for all critical decisions they will make on behalf of the organization.

> *Phil was just trying to figure out where to take his business, and the weekends were the only time to work on his business plan. "Do I have a Vision Statement?" he read aloud. "I don't have time for that stuff. I'm just trying to pay the bills and keep the lights on in the store!" The recent economic downturn impacted Phil's initial growth plans, but he was still turning a small profit and was looking to expand his brand.*

Operational
Implementation

Vision

←— Stage 1

Scope

This is a familiar refrain among many small business owners. They are faced with the reality of the aftermath of the economic downturn, new rules of engagement between business and government with the financial industry managing forward movement while still keeping a cautious eye on global markets. News media continuously bombard us with every tweak and turn on the financial and regulatory front while at the same time, most business owners do not regularly review the reason they started their business in the first place. Rather, if they are in business for several years, their mindset is typically focused on survival.

This is not to say focusing on survival is a bad thing, but it is not the only thing. As I take business owners through the visioning process, I find they renew the initial zeal and passion they held for their business. Only now it is captured in a meaningful, and very visible, way so it acts as a constant reminder of where they are going. I often liken a Vision to the North Star the sailors of old used to navigate the open seas. Through storms and other distractions, the North Star was a constant they knew would give them reliable reference for their journey. Amid the distractions of running a business in today's dynamic and uncertain environment, a well-crafted vision provides the same value.

*As a high school English teacher, a Vision and five-year outlook weren't part of Chrissy's day-to-day thinking. However, as she pondered the value of a Vision Statement, it seemed to shed new light on the recent funding challenges the organization faced. With the next board meeting only a week away, she had an opportunity to bring this up with the other board members. If Visions are applicable to any type of organization, what would it look like for her organization to help them face their current funding challenges?*

Visions are aspirational in that they outline a possible future for the organization in which its stakeholders can believe. In the case of not-for-profit organizations, this aspect of the Vision is often confused with a

Mission Statement. I have yet to work with a not-for-profit organization that did not have a Mission Statement (more on that in Chapter 2), but very few who have meaningful Vision Statements. The prevailing conversation goes something like, "I can see where a Vision would help a for-profit business, but we have a Mission Statement for the non-profit I support so I don't see the value of a Vision Statement. They are redundant in my mind." A good many organizations make the same assumption, but they find in challenging times, the Mission alone does not inspire the organization like an effective Vision would. As a practical matter, I have seen the success rate for grant money applications increase among not-for-profits with meaningful Visions and Missions as opposed to those with only a Mission Statement. The addition of a Vision provides grantees tangible access to, and understanding of, the organization's aspirations and provides a clearer sense of how the organization will sustain itself.

> *Carlos is clearly troubled by recent economic and political events. It seems the organization is struggling to find its direction since the recent economic downturn. Not only had the recession hit the family-owned company hard, they were still reeling from the recent departure of several key executives. He had to admit he had not looked at their Vision since the beginning of the economic downturn because it did not seem to matter much at the time. After all, he had reasoned, the company was in survival mode so what difference would the Vision matter at that point? Now he realized he would need to take a hard look at the Vision to see if it was still relevant.*

A clear Vision helps drive change by creating a picture of a new future. An organization dealing with change in its business (which is every organization who plans to be around another year!) knows that in order to rally the organization around the new change, a compelling reason for the change must be made. Vision Statements are one of the most powerful tools available to organizational leaders to help their teams navigate change because they help create a picture of the world on the other side of the change. If there is an existing Vision, does it still conjure an image of the desired future? If no Vision exists, creating one will help the organization see beyond the status quo, the mortal enemy of effective organizational change. In the example above, Carlos realizes the existing Vision is no longer relevant because it was far too focused on North American operations. It needed to now reflect a broader scope of global aspirations and growth. Successful organizations continuously challenge their Vision to ensure it remains relevant to the stated purpose and goals the organizational leadership wants to achieve.

Visions at a corporate level tend to be more involved than those of the small and medium business (SMB) business owner based on the scope and scale of the organization. At a minimum, they describe the aspirations for the employees, customers and operational excellence of the organization. These aspirations can either be overtly stated or implied, depending on the organization. The crucial element is shared understanding within in the organization. I recall creating a Vision with a leadership team in one of my corporate assignments. We were very satisfied with the resulting Vision when we communicated it to the rest of the organization. However, consensus was mixed based on several words that were not as inspirational as the leadership team believed. After changing those few words, the organization at large was then fully on board!

The journey to business alignment begins with a meaningful Vision that inspires and paints a picture of a desired future for the organization, regardless of size or profit status. While it may take several tries to create the right Vision, it is as important as pouring a solid foundation for a house prior to building the rest of the structure.

## QUESTIONS TO CONSIDER:

1.   What business are you in?
     _____
     _____

2.   Why are you in business?
     _____
     _____

3.   If you have a Vision for your business, to what
     extent does it reflect the purpose of your business?
     _____
     _____

4.   When is the last time you reviewed the organization's Vision?
     _____
     _____

     With the leadership team and/or board of advisors?
     _____
     _____

5.   Does the Vision still evoke the same passion as it did when you
     created it?
     _____
     _____

     If not, why not?
     _____
     _____

6.   If you do not have a Vision, what is the purpose of your business?
     _____
     _____

7.   What values do you uphold as representative of your business?
     _____
     _____

# CHAPTER 2:

## "Your Mission, should you decide to accept it…"

*~ The Importance of Mission Statements.*

**THE KEY POINT:** It is not enough just to have a Vision Statement for the business. As a Vision is a statement of the organization's desired future state, the Mission Statement creates tangible statements aligned to the Vision to provide focus in the near term or two to three years in the future. These statements provide the impetus for the Strategic Objectives, which will follow in the alignment process. To craft a successful Mission Statement, it is crucial to have an understanding of the external environment and a clear sense of the business's strengths and weaknesses. The process of creating a Mission Statement is not complete until it is clearly aligned to the Vision. In other words, someone reading the Mission and Vision together would be able to clearly see how one flows from the other.

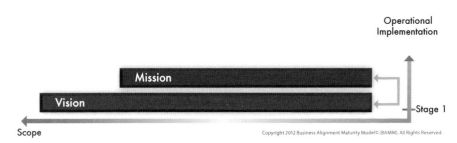

Operational
Implementation

Mission

Vision

Stage 1

Scope

A Mission Statement provides the next level of business alignment. Mission Statements are the organizational Vision Statement translated into a more tangible form. A common misconception is that Visions and Missions are the same and often get confused as such. Where the Vision provides aspiration to a business by defining its Purpose, the Mission Statement takes the intent of the Vision and translates it into tangible ideas and directives to the organization. If you had to explain to your stakeholders (your employees, investors or suppliers) the direction in which you are specifically taking your business, what would you tell them? In most cases, the Vision will not be enough to articulate your direction and intent. The Mission fulfills this role.

*Carlos's conversations with his leadership team about the Vision that was no longer relevant had naturally carried over into their corporate Mission Statement. Here too they found the Mission Statement lacking as a document meant to extract the key elements from the Vision to help create Strategic Objectives. They had come to realize the business had changed, but their focal points had not been updated to reflect those changes. Staff meetings now set aside at least thirty minutes to discuss the changes in their industry and targeted markets and to document assumptions to create a new, more relevant focus for their company.*

The Mission identifies areas the organization will focus on to work toward their stated Vision. In order to know what those areas of focus are, the organization must know what they are up against in their market and industry. The most effective tool I use to create this assessment is the External Environment Assessment, which looks outside the organizational boundaries, outside the castle gates, if you will, to assess the current environment. The areas of focus in this assessment fall into six main categories:

1. **Demographics/Psychograhics** – Influences from physical distribution and attitudinal changes of a society

2. **Economic** – Influences from financial markets and key economic indicators

3. **Political/Legal** – Influences from political processes and legislation

4. **Sociocultural** – Influences on the values, beliefs and lifestyles of a society

5. **Technical** – Influences from advances in products and services advanced through technology

6. **Global** – Influences on political, social and economic segments from globalization

All or some combination of these factors influence organizations of all types and sizes regardless of industry and location. Leaders of the organization must understand how these factors affect their operations well enough to create business assumptions, ultimately leading to a meaningful Mission Statement for the business.

The obvious question becomes, how do you stay up on all the changes in international business, politics, technology and other key areas of interest? The direct answer is the successful business owner, not-for-profit executive and corporate leader find the influencers (i.e. Thought Leaders, Emerging Competitors, Key Customers, etc.) in their industries and markets in order to monitor trends to stay on a proactive decision-making cycle. Anything less would allow others to decide what happens in your business, which is not likely to be the best direction for your organization's mission.

While the overall answer may be simply stated, the execution is much more complicated. How will you react to new mega-trends like sustainability and generational diversity? How do you know when new global competitors enter your business space? What are the costs of keeping track of new regulations and compliance? The answers to these and many more relevant questions are what every leader must factor into their development of a Mission Statement.

> *Phil was clearly sold on his new Vision for his business but was not convinced on creating a Mission Statement. He thought, "It took me a while to wrap my mind around the Vision, and I can definitely see the value as it forced me to look at why I am in this business. The Mission seems like extra work for little return." Then he realized how difficult it would be to create tangible goals from his new Vision Statement. He started to understand how a Mission Statement would give him that ability.*

Before a Mission Statement can come to life and have true meaning to the organization, the organization must know what it can reasonably accomplish. In addition to the External Environmental Assessment, one of the most useful tools in this process is the SWOT (Strengths, Weaknesses, Opportunities and Threats) Analysis. The SWOT Analysis is a point-in-time assessment of the organization against the results of the External Environmental Assessment. It helps the organization look internally at what it does well (Strengths) and what it does not do well (Weaknesses) for an overall look at what is happening within its own control. The organization then reviews the current Environmental Assessment results to identify where Strengths and Weaknesses can be externally leveraged (Opportunities) and what external obstacles (Threats) will help or hinder the organization from achieving their desired results.

A crucial aspect of the SWOT is defining "Strengths" as elements that create a competitive advantage and "Weaknesses" as elements that prevent the organization from having a competitive advantage. This additional criteria forces organizational leaders to focus on just those specific Strengths and Weaknesses which help advance the Vision and Mission in the form of a relevant Strategy.

The External Environment Assessment in concert with the SWOT Analysis enables the organization to answer a few basic questions to create or modify its Mission Statement. While there are multiple versions of the basic question set, the ones listed here capture the essence of the how the Mission Statement comes together:

- What do you do?

- How do you do it?

- For whom do you do it?

Once these become clear to the organizational leadership, a Mission Statement will begin to unfold with clear areas of value and focus for both the organization and associated stakeholders.

*Chrissy had seen how the new Vision was now taking the existing Mission in a different direction. It was drastic, as the board realized how they were too narrowly focused on their programs. She now knew how important having a clear Vision and Mission was to the Executive Director as he applied for grant money and philanthropic donations to support their program growth.*

The final piece to creating a meaningful Mission Statement is ensuring it aligns with the Vision Statement. Once the Mission Statement is completed, hold it up alongside the Vision and see if the meaning flows from Vision to Mission. Take each statement in the Mission and rationalize it against the meaning of the Vision. For instance, earlier in Chapter 1 I stated the vision Statement for RPC Leadership Associates, Inc. was "Making Leadership a Way of Life." The corresponding Mission Statement is:

- Help Organizational Leadership Teams, Business Owners and Non-Profit Boards align their Strategic Plans to improve and enhance Customer Loyalty and increase profitability.

- Help Individual Leaders improve their professional and personal performance by achieving alignment between them.

- Help Student Leaders develop their leadership potential to prepare them for the opportunities they will face as our future leaders.

Each of these three statements in the Mission was vetted against the Vision to ensure I was clear on the messaging and alignment between the two key representative statements of my business. To check for clarity, let someone who was not involved in creating the Vision or Mission (customers and suppliers work great for this task) read both documents to see if they recognize the connection. If they do, great! If not, keep refining the Mission until both the meaning and the intent are aligned.

A final thought on Vision and Mission Statements. I admittedly get some resistance when working with organizations for some of the reasons listed above as well as the iterative process involved to get it right, especially if creating one or the other for the first time. For many, this looks like an administrative process. Rather than thinking of it as an administrative process, think of it as a process validating the reason the business exists. Think of the process as a means to more clearly understand the purpose of the business as you've never understood it before. In all cases, organizations with a clear Vision as well as a clear, aligned Mission have a much better grasp of their purpose and are much better prepared to create a Strategy to compete in a very dynamic business environment.

## QUESTIONS TO CONSIDER:

8.  Do you have a mission for your business?

    _____

    _____

9.  Does it still provide the right focus for the business?

    _____

    _____

10. When is the last time you reviewed the Mission
    Statement with your team and/or board of advisors?

    _____

    _____

    What were the results?

    _____

    _____

11. How well does the organizational Mission
    Statement align with the Vision of the business?

    _____

    _____

12. How do current trends in the General Environment affect your organization through influences in:

- Demographics/Psychograhics

  _____

  _____

- Economics

  _____

  _____

- Politics/Legislation

  _____

  _____

- Socioculture

  _____

  _____

- Technology

  _____

  _____

- Globalization

  _____

  _____

13. How are you monitoring changing trends in the above areas?

  _____

  _____

14. What are the Strategic Advantages (Strengths) of your business?

  _____

  _____

  How do you know?

  _____

  _____

15.    What are the Strategic Disadvantages (Weaknesses) of your business?

_____

_____

How do you know?

_____

_____

16.    What Opportunities are you prepared to
       take competitive advantage of right now?

_____

_____

17.    What Threats are preventing you from improving
       your competitive advantage right now?

_____

_____

18.    If you do not have a Mission Statement,
       how would you answer these questions?

   •   What do you do?

_____

_____

   •   How do you do it?

_____

_____

   •   For whom do you do it?

_____

_____

19.    What are you trying to accomplish over the next 2-3 years with your business?

_____

_____

# Section 1

# CHAPTER 3:

**"…what none can see is the strategy out of which victory is evolved."**

*~ Sun Tzu, "The Art of War"*

**THE KEY POINT:** Achieving the next Stage in the Model requires aligning the organization's Strategy with the Vision and Mission. When an organization's operational environment changes (and it always does!), these three elements must be reviewed for relevance, one against the other, to ensure Stage 2 Alignment. This is especially true of the Strategy with its direct link to how and with whom the organization competes. As industry competitors change and/or new competitors arrive in the marketplace (and they always do!), the organizational Strategy must change or it quickly becomes irrelevant in today's fast moving business environment.

Strategy guides organizations to operate in ways that help them gain a sustainable advantage over their competitors. Simply stated, it is a reflection of how the organization competes in the markets and industries in which they are engaged.

*For Carlos, it was apparent the competitive landscape had changed as some of his customers had to close their doors or merge with other companies. Another customer segment shifted their business to overseas suppliers to reduce expenses. While their existing strategy of leveraging a strong distribution network was still sound, it was clear to him and his leadership team that their over-reliance on a domestic strategy was untenable. Their current international business was less than 20% of their overall revenue, but growing year over year, while at the same time the domestic revenue as a percentage of the overall revenue was declining over the same period.*

With a thorough environmental assessment and a meaningful Mission in place, it is important to determine the key strategic objectives for competing in the current business cycle. According to Harvard Business School Professor Michael Porter[1], a recognized leading authority on company strategy and their competitiveness, organizations essentially have three choices when determining their competitive strategy. They can:

- Compete on cost leadership

- Compete on their product and/or service differentiation

- Compete through a focused segmentation strategy in a narrow market segment

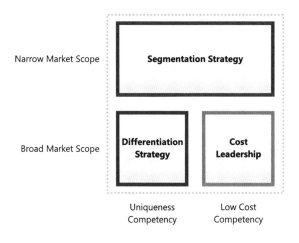

Most organizations will ultimately focus on one of the above competitive strategies, although a few have achieved success through competing in a combination of the basic strategies. In creating the organization's prevailing strategy, it is also important to understand how it translates to an international context, as Carlos does in the example above, or in a virtual online context, as you will see Phil does in the example below. For most organizations, it boils down to identifying the basic strategy most relevant to their current competitive strengths and weaknesses. They then create strategic objectives that enable the organization to leverage their competitive strengths to the market in a unique and relevant way.

*When he started the business, Phil viewed his competition as other retail outlets like his. His customers liked the face to face interaction and discussions he often had with them on how to stay active and healthy into their 60s and 70s. However, he also noticed his clients in their 50s spent less time in his store and subsequently were buying less over time. It was through the review of his competitors he realized he'd completely overlooked those who market and sell online. As he did not yet provide the ability to purchase his products online, these online competitors had free reign of younger prospects more apt to research and buy online than they were to go to a storefront to buy what they needed.*

In Chapter 2, we introduced the key aspects of the Strengths and Weaknesses in the SWOT Analysis. These aspects must be identified as strengths that provide a competitive advantage and weaknesses that create potential competitive disadvantages. These are important distinctions when creating strategic objectives that align with the Vision and Mission. The organization's strengths may not provide an ability to approach the market with a unique strategy. A common objection I hear, especially from business owners who typically have many competitors in their local area, is how there really isn't a difference in their services therefore they default to a "lower-cost" strategy. Business owners like Phil can offset this thinking by objectively and systematically assessing themselves and their environment to find the core competencies they can leverage to their competitive advantage even if that advantage is the unique skills they themselves possess. So, much like Phil realizes his weakness is lack of an online presence, his strategic objectives would now include creating an online retail presence as well as more actively marketing the business through social media to promote an "online-to-offline" (O2O) strategy.

> *Earlier, Chrissy was adamant about how her not-for-profit organization did not have competitors because they were the only organization in the area providing their unique services for teens. However, she now knows every other not-for-profit in her area of operations is a competitor for dollars and donors. Because most of the organization's revenue (over half) came from the budget coffers of a state in dire financial trouble, she realized how she and the rest of the board needed to think differently about how they executed the new Vision and updated Mission. Their new strategic objectives would more clearly focus on diversifying their sources of revenue and developing strategies to grow their existing donor base.*

When the external environment changes, as many not-for-profit organizations dependent on state funds can attest, the organization cannot simply ignore the reality and "hope for the best." A favorite expression of mine is "Hope is Not a Strategy" which also happens to be the title of one of my favorite books on value-added selling by Rick Page. The once popular strategy among organizations of "last year's revenue/cost reduction plus X%" was a poor strategy in the past and an even poorer strategy in the present. Hoping the economy changes or hoping a different political environment exists does not change the fact that organizations must effectively embrace the reality that is theirs today and create strategies leveraging their core competencies to achieve their desired results.

The Strategic Thinking process is creating:

- *A Vision of a desired future*

- *A Mission that breaks that potential future into tangible and meaningful direction*

- *A Strategy identifying how the organization will compete*

As the organization completes its Strategy in alignment with the Vision and the Mission it achieves Stage 2 Business Alignment. This is the solid foundation upon which the organization will ultimately achieve its Vision.

## *QUESTIONS TO CONSIDER:*

20.    *What assumptions is your current Strategy based on?*

_____

_____

21.    *Have they changed in the last 4 months?*

_____

_____

*How do you know?*

_____

_____

22.    *When did you last review them?*

_____

_____

*What was the outcome?*

_____

_____

23.    *Who are your top three competitors?*

_____

_____

*Does your strategy account for these competitors specifically?*

_____

_____

24. *How have you communicated the Strategy to the entire organization?*

_____

_____

*If not, what is preventing you from doing so?*

_____

_____

25. *How well can you communicate the Strategy to the stakeholders in the context of the Vision and Mission?*

_____

_____

26. *What is the feedback process for knowing if your strategy is achieving its objectives?*

_____

_____

*Another Missing Piece
To Put Together...*

## Section 2 Puzzle Piece

**1. Strategic Thinking**

**2. Operational Support Elements**

3. Tactical Execution

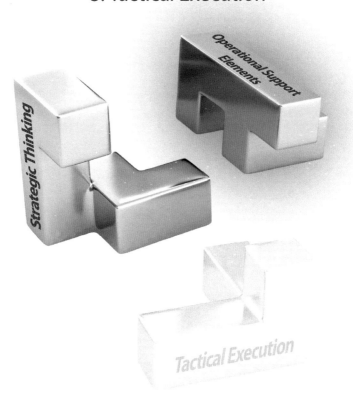

# SECTION II ~ Operational Support Elements:

# Section II: Operational Support Elements

In Section I, we discussed the Strategic Thinking Process, which, based on my experience, most executive leadership teams and non-profit boards do well. They create Visions (Stage 1 Alignment), Mission Statements and develop Strategies from those Mission Statements (Stage 2 Alignment). While I have worked with small-business owners who generally do this well, most give it a low priority, thus the reason they are a key element of focus here. The challenge with all of the above is execution. When working with organizations struggling with execution, I find they fit in one of two general categories:

- They have a strong Vision, Mission and Strategy but cannot seem to draw in the whole organization around the Strategy to achieve desired results.

- The organization posts good results at the tactical operating level but has little strategic direction, which is where many entrepreneurs find themselves when they start their business.

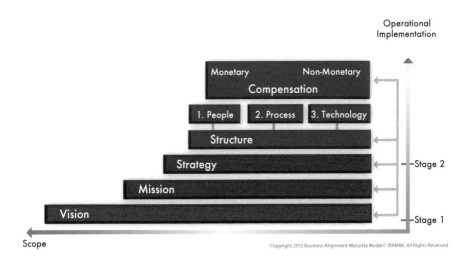

The element missing from both these groups is Operational Support, the topic of Section II. Operational Support is divided over the next two layers of The Model as Structure and Compensation. Structure is further broken down into People, Process, and Technology, in that order. Compensation is also delineated into monetary and non-monetary rewards.

Think back to the puzzle analogy in the book's introduction. At this point in the alignment process, we have the frame of the puzzle completed with all the straightedge border pieces in place. Now we group together the puzzle pieces of similar colors and patterns to help determine where they fit in the picture. In the next two layers of The Model, we explore the fit of people, processes, technology, compensation and rewards with the intention of achieving goals and Stage 3 business alignment.

So let's see how these two layers of alignment help Carlos, Chrissy and Phil with their business alignment.

# CHAPTER 4:

## "People are our most valuable asset"

*~ leveraging People, Process and Technology to achieve desired results*

**THE KEY POINT:** Many organizations, large and small, want to create a new Strategy and immediately create goals and action plans to execute the Strategy. They underestimate the challenges of executing processes that operate horizontally by people who are organized vertically. They neglect to fully re-assess their people to ensure the skills and knowledge (capability) and attitudes (compatibility) are in alignment with the new strategy. Only after they are certain they have the right people can they fully optimize their core processes to ensure the people's strengths are fully leveraged and their weaknesses mitigated. Technology support strategies are the final elements applied to avoid the common organizational traps of creating structures and automation support that are out of alignment with the Vision and Strategy.

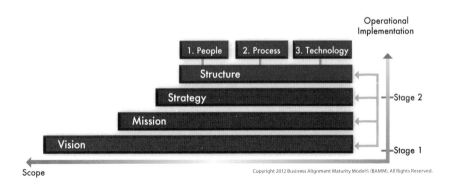

Have you ever considered the logic of fundamentally changing the organizational strategy without assessing whether the organization has the right people to execute the strategy, the right core processes to leverage the right people and the right technology support to optimize the core processes? Organizations find themselves at this crossroad after they spend a great deal of time in their strategic thinking process. They then create goals to achieve the strategy and communicate the goals to the organization. Unfortunately, they are skipping crucial pieces of the alignment process by going direct from Strategy to Goals. By skipping these crucial pieces, they handicap their strategy and their enthusiasm will soon give way to frustration with the execution.

A crucial element of the business alignment process is aligning the organizational structure to the strategy. Within the structure layer lie additional alignment challenges and opportunities, especially as the organization grows in size. People in an organization are typically organized vertically to support management control requirements. However, the processes they execute flow horizontally from start to finish. For example, a typical service implementation process begins with a signed order and horizontally moves through the organization ends with an invoice for services. Along the way, the process crosses multiple vertically structured organizations (sales, project management, engineering and billing to name a few) which all have their own set of rules and control mechanisms. This combination of vertical and horizontal dependencies creates enough complexity to throw the business "out-of-alignment" if not managed effectively.

*Carlos sat in his office having just returned from the first budget meeting with the senior leadership team. As he and the team discussed the Vision, Mission and Strategy in the context of making changes in the business, a startling reality surfaced. It was clear some of the senior staff were not on board with the changes in direction. Others were on board with the changes, but he could tell they were struggling with how they might be implemented. He couldn't help but recall the spirited debates over operational and financial goals that seemed to go nowhere. Now sitting in his office, he pondered the situation and how best to approach it.*

One of the first questions Carlos needs to ask himself is whether the company is looking to execute their new strategy with the same personnel organization they had before the new Vision, Mission and Strategy were created. Experience tells me this question is either missed altogether or is a sub-task delegated to the Human Resources department. There is an expression we hear often which goes, "What got you here, won't necessarily get you there." An organization's previous strategy and structure got them where they are today, but is it safe to assume the old structure supports the new strategy in a way that will achieve their new desired results? It is here in the process that I often hear statements like, "We have great people here" or "Our culture is very people centric and we pride ourselves in our ability to achieve our desired results." It is not really a question of having great people as much as it is having the right great people.

To illustrate the point, let's draw a 2x2 grid and label the left axis "Compatibility" and the bottom axis "Capability" as shown in Figure 4.1. We will label each one with a Low to High range of values on both the left and bottom axis.

*Figure 4.1*

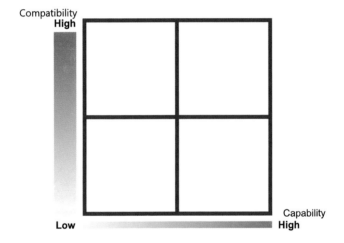

While there are variations to this model (for instance a 3x3 grid for more granularity), we will use the 2x2 to make the overall point here.

Every employee in the organization is assessed on their capability to execute their roles in the organization. They must have the crucial skills and knowledge to contribute to the organization in a way that achieves the organization's desired results. They are also assessed on their compatibility with the culture and values of the organization; does their attitude support the strategy? I will typically ask an organization,

"What percentage of success does each of these represent?" Most will answer 60% to 70% Capability and 30% to 40% Compatibility. In fact, it is nearly 75% Compatibility (attitude) and 25% Capability (skills and knowledge). Skills alone account for less than 5% of overall success. So, the first challenge is making sure the organization has the right people to achieve the **new** desired results.

In any organization, you will find a distribution of Compatibility and Capability represented in the diagram by the Xs in each quadrant of Figure 4.2. These Xs represent the different combinations of employees most organizations will have.

Figure 4.2

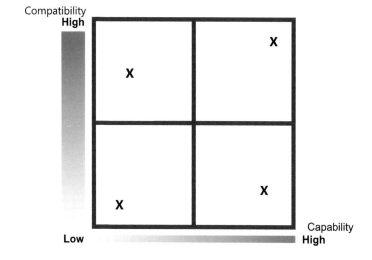

Those in the Low Compatibility and Low Capability to the new strategy will weigh down the ability to achieve success and must be managed decisively to either a new role in the organization or new opportunities outside the organization. Those on the opposing quadrant who are High Compatibility and High Capability relative to the new strategy will likely be the change agents for the organization.

Those in the organization who are High Compatibility and Low Capability relative to the new strategy become opportunities for targeted training and development. Because these associates are a cultural fit (75% of success), the investment in additional skills and knowledge is a high payoff win-win solution. The final group, those who are High Capability but Low Compatibility to the new strategy present the greatest challenge to the organization. Because this group has demonstrated an ability to produce results in the past, the fact they are cultural mismatches tends to be overlooked. Rationalization kicks in with discussions that sound like "They can really sell," "He/She is a great engineer" or "They have a wealth of knowledge about the product." While all of these may well be true, because they are identified as Low Compatibility, they will be obstacles to success unless their attitude changes to embrace the new strategy.

*"When was the last time we assessed our board and staff?" Chrissy wondered aloud. Her mind was racing through some of the more recent one-on-one conversations and board meeting discussions that caused her to realize they were dealing with board members who were resisting the changes being considered for the non-profit organization.*

To illustrate the challenge and opportunity of having the right people in the organization to execute the new strategy, let's go back to the original diagram (Figure 4.2) and expand it to reflect the new strategy. We will use the same 2x2 grid and we will shift it to reflect a new standard (raising the bar, if you will) for both compatibility and capability. Our new diagram looks like the one found on the next page. (Figure 4.3)

*Figure 4.3*

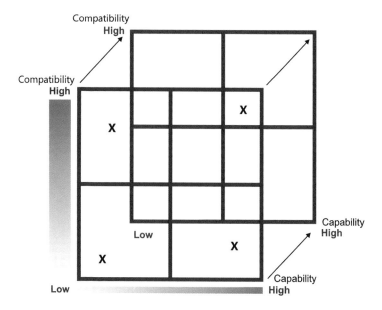

As we look at the people represented by the original Xs in the first diagram, we now see that someone in the top right quadrant in the original diagram might now be barely in the upper right quadrant of the new diagram. They may very well end up in the lower left quadrant if they do not evolve with the new Vision, Mission and Strategy.

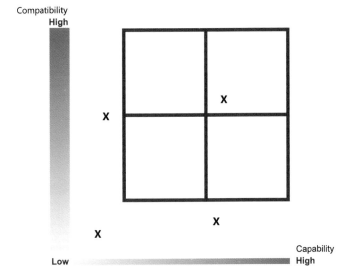

The new quadrants represent the Compatibility and Capabilities required to execute the new strategy and are represented in Figure 4.4 as we strip away the old strategy.

If we look at the example from the original quadrants, we see three of the four representative employees from the original assessment now sit outside the new quadrants. The fourth, a high performer in the original strategy is average against the new strategy. The organization must assess its people, beginning with the senior leadership team, to see if they are Compatible (relevant) and Capable enough for the new organizational direction.

The next element in the Structural alignment is Process. Process follows People in The Model so you can create processes that leverage the strengths of your people rather than trying to leverage the wrong people into existing processes. During my most recent process improvement certification, my instructor amplified this relationship between people and process this way, "Poor processes will ruin good people; Good processes magnify good people".

Alignment in this stage starts with identifying the organization's core processes. W. Edwards Deming, who many consider the penultimate authority on the field of Quality Management said, "If you can't describe what you are doing as a process, you don't know what you're doing." In most cases, core processes are those that produce the most direct value to the organization, whether it be for-profit such as Carlos's situation or not-for-profit as in Chrissy's case.

There are generally five core processes that apply to every organization. They are:

- Inbound Logistics/Taking Orders

- Operations/Manufacture Product

- Outbound Logistics/Deliver Product

- Marketing and Sales

- Service/Maintain the Customer

Processes such as Administration, HR, IT, Purchasing, Legal, etc., are supporting processes that, by definition, support the core processes.

For example, a retail operation's core processes would be: Partner with Vendors, Purchase Goods, Inventory Management, Store Operations and Marketing and Sales. An Engineering Services firm may have: R&D, Engineering, Designs and Solutions, Marketing and Sales and Service. These are the processes that have priority to an effectively aligned business.

When the strategy changes, every business has to assess the people first and then the processes they use. The people have to be the right people capable of achieving the goals that align with the Strategy.

With the right people on board, do your core processes optimize your peoples' strengths? By understanding what the organization's core processes are and matching them to the right people, the organization achieves what Jim Collins[1] describes in his book *Good to Great* as putting the right people on the right seats on the bus. Having the right people performing the key functions relevant to the organization now and in the future, will ensure sustainable success.

> *"This might be a problem," Phil muttered to himself as he stared at the spreadsheet he created reflecting his assessment of his employees. He made a list of skills, knowledge and attitudes he needed from his employees to execute a new web-based strategy. As he stared at the numbers he used to reflect his assessments, his eyes kept moving back to his assessment of his staff's technical skills, which by his measure were weak across the board. All his staff members are Baby Boomers who are very much in sync with the purpose of his business. However, he had his doubts about their technical skills based on his observations of their use of the store computers. Two of the three seemed interested in wanting to learn while the third was openly opposed to learning anything new reasoning it had no bearing on his ability to do his current job.*

While it is true for any business, a small business owner with only a few employees cannot assume what got them to this point will get them where they want to go without making some adjustments. In Phil's case, once he assesses his people and core processes, he must provide supporting technology to make it all work effectively.

The third component of Structure is the supporting technology that enables the core processes to perform optimally while, again, supporting the ability of people to achieve desired results. The order in which technology falls in this layer is important in that it is applied to support core processes. Far too many organizations see technology as a replacement for core processes rather than a support. Consider the organization that puts people first, then processes, then technology.

Typically they leverage technology to replace routine supporting processes (those that are not core to the business) in an effort to free their people to continue to provide value to the business. However, those organizations that view the relationship in reverse (Technology-Process-People) find themselves in a decision-making cycle where they implement technology to replace core processes, modify the processes to fit the technology and try to dovetail people into supporting roles to the technology. We see plenty of examples of this in retail, for example, when companies replace their core selling process with self-service web-based systems. While self-service web services can be valuable, live customer support is often non-existent when an exception or an issue arises in the retail sales process. Customer Service is a core process in today's global economy. In an environment where multiple companies worldwide replicate products and services, the differentiator becomes the ability to create a meaningful customer experience. Technology must enable the customer to have a complete and satisfying experience or they will simply choose the competitor.

People, Process and Technology all work hand-in-hand to set the stage for the organizational strategy to deliver the desired results. They are managed in this order so as to avoid placing the organization's most valuable asset, its compatible and capable people, in a supporting role that minimizes their ability to create value for the organization's stakeholders.

## QUESTIONS TO CONSIDER:

27.   To what extent are the people's skills and knowledge in
      your organization still relevant to the current strategy?

      _____

      _____

      How do you know?

      _____

      _____

28.   To what extent are the attitudes in the organization
      compatible with the purpose and culture?

      _____

      _____

      How do you know?

      _____

      _____

29.   To what extent do performance management and recruiting
      practices reflect and fully support your current Strategy?

      _____

      _____

30.   To what extent does your organization fully understand
      what the core processes of the organization are?

      _____

      _____

31.   To what extent is your organization structured around your
      core processes?

      _____

      _____

32. *To what extent do your core processes leverage your peoples' strengths?*

   _____

   _____

   *How do you know?*

   _____

   _____

33. *How does your organization's technology infrastructure fully support the efficiency of your core processes?*

   _____

   _____

34. *How is your technology enabling the strengths of your people?*

   _____

   _____

# CHAPTER 5:

## "What's my Motivation?"

~ *How do monetary and non-monetary compensation/*
*rewards influence alignment?*

**THE KEY POINT:** Compensation and Rewards are crucial to the alignment process by influencing the behaviors crucial to success in any organization. They consist of both monetary and non-monetary solutions and can be a combination of formal and informal programs. Of significance are those solutions that promote job satisfaction versus those that merely eliminate job dissatisfaction. All too often, organizations rely heavily on the two most common externally applied motivators: rewards and fear. However, a third motivator, attitude, is recognized as the only true long-term motivator. The sooner organizations recognize positive attitudes as the only effective long-term motivation, the quicker they achieve desired results.

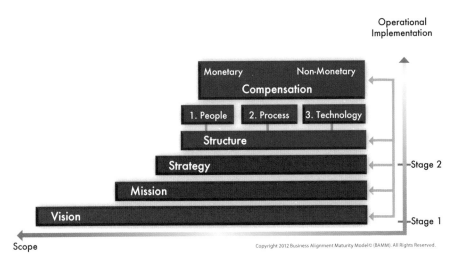

Having the right compensation and/or rewards systems in place is crucial to achieving desired results. Motivation is a powerful influence on success, especially during times of change, so it must be overtly addressed and understood.

*Phil knew his employees were very attentive to their customers and seemed very knowledgeable about whatever the customers were asking them about. However, he did have some concerns about their ability to adjust to change when he mentioned his new online strategy. While they seem to be in agreement, he sensed they felt threatened by the changes. He knew when they heard their kids and grandkids talk about Facebook, Twitter, Flickr, etc. they did not have a clue what they were talking about. It seemed to him whenever the conversation turned to addressing a younger audience in the business, they would tense up as if they felt less relevant. He was struggling with how to motivate them through the changes he needed to make.*

In my own experience with organizations, large or small, dealing with the challenge of resistance to change, the immediate thoughts go to money. While compensation programs need to be addressed in any organization, they do not always have to be based solely on money. In fact, studies show that in high performing organizations, money is rarely one of the top three reasons why the organization performs as well as it does. This is not to downplay the importance of having a viable and competitive compensation structure but to understand the importance of having both monetary and non-monetary based compensation and rewards programs.

Another way to view the relationship between monetary and non-monetary programs is to understand what Frederick Herzberg[1] posited in the late 1960s when he made the distinction between those factors that eliminate job dissatisfaction but do not necessarily promote job satisfaction (Hygiene Factors) and those factors that foster job satisfaction (Motivator Factors). His Two-Factor theory is depicted below.

Hygiene Factors would be Company Policy and Administration, Wages and Salaries, Quality of Supervision and/or Inter-personal Relations, Working Conditions and Feelings of Job Security. These are factors that prevent dissatisfaction and must not be confused with elements that promote job satisfaction and engagement. You can also see these are factors based primarily on tangible things an employee can see and sense in the here and now.

Motivator Factors, on the other hand, are Status, Opportunity for Advancement, Recognition, Responsibility, Challenging/Stimulating Work, Sense of Personal Achievement and Personal Growth. These are the factors that actively promote job satisfaction and employee engagement. While less tangible than Hygiene Factors, they provide a powerful motivator for satisfying an employee's intrinsic value of worth to the organization. It is incumbent upon organizational leaders to understand what these factors are relative to their organizations and ensure they are not leveraging Hygiene Factors and expecting the results of Motivator Factors. So, while a fair compensation program and its associated programs (bonuses, merit increases, variable compensation, etc.) will certainly have value to the organization's overall well being, leaders must also look at what they can do that is not strictly monetary in nature.

*Chrissy was thinking about last night's board meeting and wondering aloud what motivated some of the board members. Since their board members are all volunteers, their motivation to serve on the board had to be based on their emotional connection to the Vision. The same had to be true of their staff. Even though they were in paid positions, the key to their motivation rested on how they address their passion for the Mission. It seemed to Chrissy staff motivation is more of a challenge now that they had more of an age-diverse board and staff as each age group seems to have very different needs for motivation.*

Intrinsic rewards programs are often a difficult process to formalize. Everyone has a different set of motivators that helps them determine how much energy, direction and persistence they will put forth in support of the organization's strategy. Leadership must find the right mix of motivators for their respective teams to help them work through the continuous changes while keeping them fully engaged in the future of the organization. It cannot be done simply applying management practices. Most management practices fall into the Hygiene Factors and do not evoke the emotional investment needed by members of the organization to fully achieve sustainable success much like the scenario with Chrissy above. Leaders are the ones who can create the environment for Motivator Factors to take hold and provide a culture of sustainable success.

> Carlos was reviewing the assessment reports for his top thirty-five executives. The report provided him with information specific to the executive team's collective communications effectiveness and their prevailing motivators. He could not help but notice their primary motivators were spread across the seven different categories of motivation in the assessment. He even noticed how his Chief Operating Officer had a few different motivators than he did.

It is not always obvious what one's motivators really are. While studies like the ones that generated the previously mentioned Herzberg's Two Factor Theory provide a wealth of information about what might be, it is not until an organization applies the theory to their real set of circumstances that progress can take place. Individual assessments such as the Values Index based on the studies of Dr. Eduard Spranger and Gordon Allport or organizational level assessments like the Organizational Culture Inventory (OCI) can provide a wealth of information around employee satisfaction and engagement and the impact of current monetary and non-monetary compensation programs.

## QUESTIONS TO CONSIDER:

35.   *To what extent are your current monetary
      compensation/rewards programs effective?*

      _____

      _____

      *How do you know?*

      _____

      _____

36.   *What attitudes and behaviors do your
      monetary compensation/rewards promote?*

      _____

      _____

      *How do you know?*

      _____

      _____

37.   *What attitudes and behaviors do you want your
      monetary compensation/rewards to promote?*

      _____

      _____

38.   *What non-monetary rewards programs are in place?*

      _____

      _____

39. *What attitudes and behaviors do your non-monetary compensation and reward programs promote?*

_____

_____

*How do you know?*

_____

_____

40. *What attitudes and behaviors do you want your non-monetary compensation and rewards programs to promote?*

_____

_____

## And Now We're Putting All
## The Missing Pieces Together...

**Section 3 Puzzle Piece**

# 1. Strategic Thinking

# 2. Operational Support Elements

### 3. Tactical Execution

# Section III
# ~ Tactical Execution:

# *Section III: Tactical Execution*

In Section I, we introduced the first two Stages of Operational Maturity in The Model (Vision Statement and a cohesive Strategy). In Section II, we discussed the key elements necessary to achieve the next two levels of Alignment (People, Process, Technology and Compensation/Rewards). Each layer in The Model is crucial in its own right. However, they are even more crucial when addressed in relation to each other and the layers before and after them in The Model. We will now introduce the final three layers of The Model. We begin with Goals and their role in executing the Strategy to achieve Stage 3 Alignment. We will introduce the importance of Scientific Methods used to capture the data and leverage it to achieve the Goals. And finally, achieving Stage 4 Alignment through the execution of all previous layers to achieve desired results.

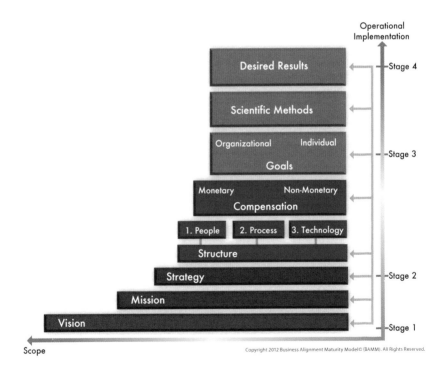

# CHAPTER 6:

## "Goals are dreams with deadlines."

*~ the importance of goals in achieving desired results*

**THE KEY POINT:** Setting Goals and achieving Desired Results is crucial to a leader's success regardless of the organization they lead. The goal planning process defines key steps to ensure goals are set in place and effectively executed. Documenting the rewards (or consequences) of achieving the goal (or not) provides the underlying urgency to complete the goal. Identifying the potential obstacles up front, along with associated solutions and action steps, reduces unnecessary rework and costly time spent reacting to events that likely should have been accounted for up front. Documenting the people accountable for each action step with an associated completion date completes the accountability trail prior to identifying a completion date for the overall goal.

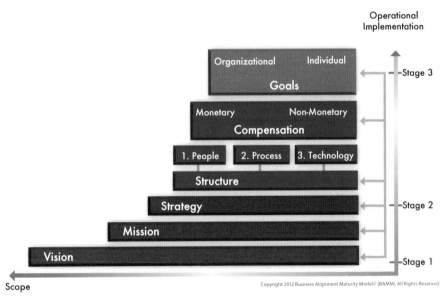

The organizational goal setting process typically consists of the leadership team reviewing each of the major components (or objectives/strategies/planks as they are sometimes referred to in larger organizations) of their strategy. The team creates goals for how they will approach each component in the strategy. They then agree on the complete set of organizational goals for the year.

*"The budgeting process seems to be going well for now," Carlos thought to himself. He and his team had reviewed the results of the leadership assessments and evaluations from previous meetings and were now looking at the goals for the organization. Ironically, it seemed to him to be a more productive process now that they better understand their people, process and technology capabilities. The budget process now included conversations around their ability to support their goals. The question on his mind now was how to determine which goals to focus on.*

Most organizational leaders are generally good at goal setting. They are able to create a set of goals they believe will advance the organization in some way. The challenge becomes the associated execution of the goals to achieve the desired results. It starts with the relative clarity of the goals in the first place. Most organizations understand the value of SMART (Specific, Measurable, Attainable, Realistically High and Time-bound) Goals. However, there are several other key elements that make goals even more relevant to the organization's strategy. The goals must also be written and visible, aligned with the organization's strategy and have a sense of ownership. We abbreviate these new elements as WAY (Written, Aligned and Yours). Thus the new acronym for effective goals becomes WAY-SMART.

It is one thing to establish a goal. It is another thing to establish the relative importance of that goal. If the rewards for achieving the goal are not compelling or the consequences of not achieving the goal are mediocre and less severe, then the energy the organization puts behind the goal will be lackluster. Being able to communicate an organizational goal with "We need to achieve X so we can increase market share by Y" or "We need to achieve X or we will need to reduce expenses by Y" are powerful motivators to achieving goals and thus should be explicitly communicated to the organization.

In addition to clear communication, it is imperative to understand the potential obstacles to achieving desired results before setting off toward

*Chapter 6: Goals*

the goal. Being a licensed pilot, I often use an example of a pilot flying to another destination by getting in the cockpit, starting the plane and taking off in the general direction of the destination. Would you fly with that pilot? Of course not! Someone like that should not be allowed to fly. In fact, Federal Aviation Administration regulations prevent pilots from doing just that. However, there are no regulations to prevent business leaders and/or owners from doing the very same thing with their business strategies. They only focus on the final destination. Businesses often launch strategies and associated goals without explicitly looking at the possible obstacles in their way ahead of time. It is as if they focus only on the expected outcome and hope that all the elements line up accordingly. In today's business environment, hope is never a viable strategy. Just like the pilot needs to check the weather, the terrain and other air traffic along their route, so too do business leaders need to check the business environment to see what obstacles might prevent them from achieving their goals.

Have you ever had to correct the direction of a goal halfway to completion? It probably happens more often than you would like. How often does your response to those situations sound something like "… but that's just the way it goes, isn't it?" When those situations occur, how much effort is it to get headed back in the right direction? It is typically a frustrating exercise because of the rework and reaction time required to get the goal back on track. In an ever-changing business environment, constantly shifting resources to react to unanticipated changes can be a gross waste of time and money. At this point you might be thinking, "We can't anticipate every issue that will hit us in the next year." If your organization has already completed earlier elements of The Model (assessing the external environment, SWOT Analysis, etc.) then you have identified some of the high level obstacles in the form of weaknesses and threats. While there is no perfect system to anticipate what those future issues will be, asking yourself what the possible obstacles might be to achieving specific goals and creating viable solutions to those obstacles proactively will reduce the amount of time and money you expend reactively.

Engaging the right people in the organization is also crucial. Whether you have thirty-five leaders at the top of your organization like Carlos or three employees like Phil below, fully engaging all of them in the goal setting process will likely uncover the vast majority of potential obstacles. I would venture to say, if all key leaders and/or associates had some input to the goal setting process, including what the possible obstacles and associated solutions would be, most of the potential obstacles would be captured.

One of the most common points of resistance I hear to leveraging this idea is misinterpreting the identification of potential obstacles as overall resistance to change. In some cases, that is exactly what it may be. Much like professional salespeople who know the difference between an objection and a stall, so too must a leader understand the difference between identifying obstacles and resistance to change. Proper facilitation of the discussion and leveraging the previous elements of The Model will help articulate which you are facing.

Identifying the potential obstacles now requires solutions to overcoming each one. When I learned to fly in Alaska, the mountains were obstacles for nearly every flight I took. Not only do some of the mountains exceed the altitude my plane could fly, but their height also generated weather patterns that were different at the base of the mountain than at the mountain's peak. Clearly my choice of solutions did not include flying over them, so I needed to plan my flight path around them as necessary. Doing so changes the resources (time, fuel, etc.) required to complete the flight. In most cases, there were several possible solutions to each obstacle that I would consider before choosing the one that made the most sense for that flight.

Business obstacles in front of organizational leaders present a similar challenge. Identifying multiple solutions to each obstacle creates a cache of solutions to achieve the desired results. Each of these possible solutions can be weighed against their own set of pros and cons to determine which works best to overcome each specific obstacle. You will likely have similar possible solutions to other obstacles giving you some economy of scale in determining best possible solutions overall.

> *The whole process of looking at his team's capabilities, compatibilities and motivation moved Phil to make an effort to more actively involve his team in the planning process for the business. As the team gathered in the back of the store, Phil quietly reminded himself to be open to the obstacles and solutions they would raise. An open mind was important to effective positive change, and he felt ready to move forward. After consolidating related obstacles into categories, they were able to spend the remaining time brainstorming possible solutions to the obstacles as well as documenting specific action steps to implement each solution. Two hours later, Phil and his team stepped back to review the notes on five full flip chart pages taped to the wall. "Great job folks!" He enthusiastically addressed the team. "What did you think of the process so far?" "So far?" replied his office manager, "What else is there?"*

"The devil is in the details" as the expression goes. Solutions require Action Steps to be executable. Determining these action steps is crucial to achieving desired results because they become the specific actionable elements of the goal. Because they are actionable, action verbs are used to describe the steps to take in enough detail to be clearly understood in purpose and intent. Statements that begin with words like: deliver, document, create, implement are but a few examples of words that denote some definitive action will occur. These action steps should be placed on individual and group calendars so each step retains meaning over the course of time and is equally understood by everyone it impacts. Even after establishing action steps for each solution to overcome the obstacles, the process is still not complete.

> *"Rough week at school?" Chrissy's husband asked, as she was clearly deep in thought. "No, school wasn't any more of a week than normal. Actually, it was the board meeting last night. We were talking about our specific action steps for next year's goals, which everyone seemed to be on board with. However, when we got to the part where we needed to assign specific owners and completion dates to the board members, the conversation did not go as well. It seems we have board members who are comfortable coming up with ideas but not as comfortable putting their name on the line and/or committing to a completion date. Several even stated because they were volunteers to the organization, it was inappropriate to hold them accountable for organizational goals."*

Action steps are often meaningless without having a completion date and someone who is, by name, accountable for ensuring the action step is completed. The completion date of the action step is crucial in establishing a timeline for completing key activities in the overall goal achievement. Depending on the organizational goal, it is likely there are interdependencies across business units or organizations within the organization to achieve that goal. These dependencies arise when multiple groups or teams are using similar resources or are connected to each other by virtue of being part of the same process or processes. Action step completion dates help manage the time and resources required to accomplish each step. In a larger project or organizational goal, an action step may become a WAY-SMART Goal by itself and the process repeats itself at a more detailed level than before.

By setting action step completion dates, the combined set of dates allows the goal completion date to become clearer. How many times have organizations or individuals set goals and arbitrarily set a completion date for the goals? This is the process that usually ends up being re-worked as described earlier in this chapter. However, when obstacles are identified up front and actions are assigned completion dates, a more rational overall completion date materializes.

Someone must be identified by name (as opposed to by team, department or business unit) as accountable for the completion of each action step. It will be far less clear who will accomplish a task if this person is only identified as "Marketing Committee" or "Engineering Department" as opposed to "Mike Nelson" or "Sue Jones."

If, as in the previous example of Chrissy's board, members fail to take accountability for action steps, go back to the members' Capability and Compatibility assessments. With the previous discussions of People in Chapter 4, it should become apparent how the people and goals alignment made sense to connect these two in a quantifiable way. It begs the question, "Do we really have the right people in the organization and are our goals aligned with what our teams/board/staff can and need to do?"

Stage 3 Alignment occurs when the organizational goals as well as the associated individual goals are in sync with the Strategy. They are executed complementary to others in the business rather than at cross-purposes to others in the business. The goals are vetted through the lens of People, Process and Technology to optimize success and are supported by Compensation and Rewards which drive the motivation to achieve the goals.

## QUESTIONS TO ASK:

41. How would you describe your goal-setting process to a complete stranger?

_____

_____

42. Are your Goals WAY-SMART (Written, Aligned, Yours, Specific, Measurable, Attainable, Realistically High and Time Bound)?

_____

_____

43. How would describe your process for documenting the Rewards for accomplishing the goal and the Consequences of NOT achieving the goal?

_____

_____

44. What is your process to identify and document the multiple potential obstacles that could derail the goal(s)?

_____

_____

45. What is the process for creating possible solutions to overcome each potential obstacle?

_____

_____

46. What is your process to document action steps with associated accountable people and a completion date for each action step?

_____

_____

47. How do the action steps completion dates and the overall completion date of the goal align?

_____

_____

# CHAPTER 7:

## "An organization does well what their leaders measure."

*~ more than just what you measure but also how you measure it?*

**THE KEY POINT:** Having goals does little for an organization if they cannot measure their progress. Deciding what to measure is important to the alignment process as it, in conjunction with rewards, ensures behavior is aligned with desired results. Using the Balanced Scorecard is one way to measure success. However, just as important to what you measure is HOW you measure goals. Look at your process for extracting the data necessary to measure your key goals (think current sales revenue or current donor revenue). It must be a seamless process aligned with your goals and enable you as a leader to make real-time, knowledge-based decisions to create progress. If how you measure key goals is onerous, the metrics will lose importance and ultimately lose value to your business.

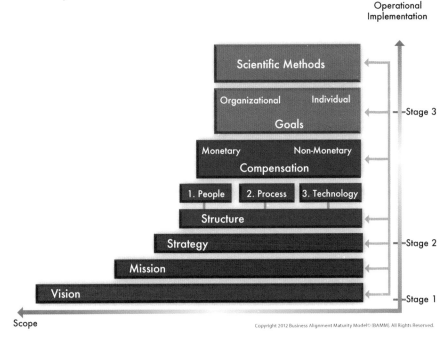

What is your methodology for determining what to measure? How do you determine what the key metrics will be so your strategy stays in alignment? More specifically, how do you determine the balance of metrics so you maintain a sense of equilibrium between your financial results, your operational results and what your customers and employees are saying about the business?

> *Carlos was on his way back to his office having just left a meeting with the COO and the CFO. With the new Strategy and Goals in place, they now turned their attention to the details around the process of gauging their success. The leadership team created a solid mix of financial and operational metrics. Upon reflection, he could not say the same about customer- and employee-based metrics. They created a few customer related metrics, but he was at a loss to recall employee related metrics. He thought to himself, "We have a robust set of metrics for financial and operational results, but now that I think about it, our metrics around customer and employee focus are not as robust as we would like."*

While there are many methodologies for measuring the organization's achievement of desired results, the one I found to be the most flexible across multiple industries and business operations is the Balanced Scorecard. Developed by Drs. Robert Kaplan and David Norton[1] in the 1990s, the Balanced Scorecard promotes a balanced measurement of four crucial areas to any business operation as seen in Figure 7.1 below.

*Figure 7.1*

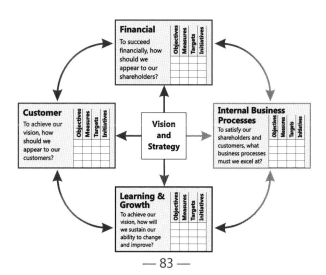

It is born from the premise that financial measurements alone do not tell the complete story of the business in its full context. Other areas of the business (large or small, for-profit or non-profit) are drivers of the financial results and are just as important for making sound, knowledge-based decisions. The interdependencies between the four areas of the Balanced Scorecard enable leaders to better understand the complexities of cause-and-effect in achieving overall business alignment. The fours perspectives are detailed below:

- The Learning & Growth Perspective - This perspective includes employee development and corporate cultural attitudes related to both individual and corporate self-improvement. In a knowledge-worker organization, people -- the only repository of knowledge -- are the main resource. In the current climate of rapid technological change, it is becoming necessary for knowledge workers to be in a continuous learning mode. Measurements are put into place to guide leaders in investing training and development funds where they can help the most.

- The Business Process Perspective - This perspective refers to internal business processes. Measurements based on this perspective allow leaders to know how well their businesses are running and whether its products and services conform to customer requirements (the mission). These measurements are typically designed by those who know the organization's core processes most intimately (Chapter 4).

- The Customer Perspective - Recent management philosophy has shown an increasing focus on the importance of customer focus and customer loyalty in any business. These are leading indicators: if customers are not satisfied and loyal, they will eventually find other suppliers that will meet their needs. Poor performance from this perspective is thus a leading indicator of future decline, even when the current financial picture may look good. In developing measurements for loyalty, customers should be analyzed in terms of customer types and the processes for which the organization provides products or services to those customer groups.

- The Financial Perspective – The Balanced Scorecard still respects the traditional need for financial data. Timely and accurate funding data will always be a priority, and leaders will do whatever necessary to provide it, but the point is that too much emphasis on financials leads to the "unbalanced" situation with regard to other perspectives.

These measurements (or others using a similar balanced approach) are the difference between the strategy as a passive idea and one of active execution.

*While looking at the latest set of monthly results, it occurred to Chrissy they already had a solid set of metrics around their financials and operational programs because they needed much of the information for their ongoing grant writing and funding efforts. However, she had to admit they didn't have a good methodology for measuring their donor activity and staff development. With a twenty-two member staff, she could not necessarily assume they had a pulse on how they all feel. She thought to herself, "I cannot recall ever discussing succession planning or leadership development at any board meetings since I've been a member so that would also be an area to start measuring."*

The leading indicators versus lagging indicators comparison is another key dimension for measuring desired results. Lagging indicators are those measurements providing results of decisions made in the past. For instance, profit is a measurement of decisions made 30 to 90 days prior to the point of measurement. Additionally, there is minimal predictability, if any at all, in measuring profit. Profit can be achieved in multiple ways (increased revenue, decreased expenses or both) and the enabling operations are open to artificial stimulus (deferred payments, pre-booking orders, etc.). So once a lagging indicator is reported, it is generally too late to do anything about it or has limited value looking forward.

Leading indicators, on the other hand, do have a level of predictability to them that provides an indication of future success. Customer and/ or donor loyalty is a measurement providing an indication of future operations. An effective donor loyalty program, for example, enables the organization (like Chrissy's in the example above) to assume, with some level of confidence, the donor activity in the short term will be positive. Every organization seeking to closely manage their business alignment must have a good mix of leading and lagging indicators.

> *Phil reflected on how he and his team identified nineteen different goals for the following year. In his most recent staff meeting, his Office Manager asked how they would measure goals. Initially Phil had responded to the question using the methodology already in place to measure revenue and basic operations (product turns, inventory, etc.) but that only covered about half of the new goals. Now he had to determine an efficient means to capture the data necessary to know how they were doing on the other goals they wanted to achieve.*

The discussion on how to measure takes me back to a time when, as a corporate executive covering a large (~$1B) territory, I had a multitude of operations to measure. I had already implemented many of the concepts described in this book so far. However, during a visit to one of the offices in the region, one of my managers brought to my attention how she had to manually create 23 reports for me – every week! I was stunned at the time commitment I was asking of a team of over 40 managers and directors in order to produce the measurements of desired results. The lesson learned is for leaders to understand exactly how (i.e. the processes/methods used) they will capture and use the measurements they create.

Technology has certainly accelerated our ability to extract, organize and present data and information to multiple stakeholders in any organization. The reality, however, is only a handful of measurements need to be viewed in real or near-real time, not the 23 from my previous example. Determining which ones they are goes to the discussion of core processes in Chapter 4. Core processes, defined as those crucial to your organization and business, should always be measured in as close to real time as possible. For example I will often ask, "How easy would it be to view yesterday's sales numbers for your business?" The assumption here is sales is a core process for nearly all businesses. If business leaders can view the sales numbers easily on his or her computer or smart-phone, the organization likely has invested effectively in measurement processes. If, on the other hand, the leader must call up the sales numbers in one system, import the numbers into a stand-alone system to be organized and sorted before viewing on yet a third system, I would argue more investment is required in the measurement systems. In today's global environment, business leaders can ill afford to lag in their ability to make knowledge-based decisions to stay competitive and effectively execute their strategy.

Scientific methods encompass the ideas and methodologies that create the ability to make timely and accurate decisions about the business. With the sheer volume of information available to leaders every minute of every day, the ability to quickly get to the information they need to run their businesses provides them the knowledge to stay in alignment with their Vision and Strategy.

## *QUESTIONS TO ASK:*

48. *Are your current business measurements weighed too heavily to one or two elements of the business?*

_____

_____

49. *If so, what can you do to balance them across all key aspects of your business?*

_____

_____

50. *How do you measure progress?*

_____

_____

51. *What is your mix of leading and lagging measurements?*

_____

_____

52. *How easy is it to view a report for daily, weekly, monthly business metrics, especially for core processes like sales?*

_____

_____

53. *How much and/or how little manual intervention do you need to get the information needed to make key business decisions?*

_____

_____

54. *How much input from others in your business goes into the measurements used to run your business?*

_____

_____

# CHAPTER 8:

## "Leadership is setting goals and achieving desired results"

*~ Understanding the difference between activities and results*

**THE KEY POINT:** All the previous stages discussed in this book lead us to the key point in this chapter; Achieving Desired Results is achieving Stage 4 Alignment. We started with Stage 1 Alignment with a common Vision. Stage 2 Alignment occurs when the organization creates an effective Strategy describing how the organization will compete in their market. Stage 3 Alignment occurs when the Goals associated with the Strategy are aligned across the organization. This implies the People, Processes and supporting Technology are in alignment across the entire organization to avoid one part of the business being at cross purposes with the goals of another part of the business. Stage 4 Alignment occurs when the desired results are achieved based on the aligned Organizational Goals. It is where Effective Communication, Leadership and Organizational Culture all play a role in an organization achieving their desired results.

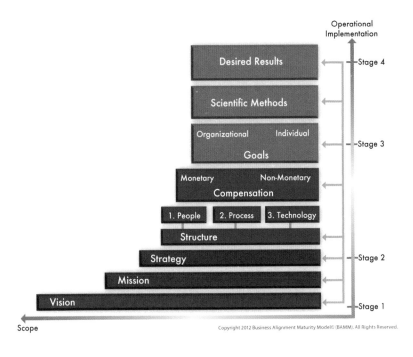

Achieving desired results is the ultimate in business success. It is never about just achieving results. It is about achieving the results that matter to the organization. It is about achieving the results that allow the organization to compete effectively in the short-term and realize its organizational vision in the long-term.

> *"Has it really been four months since the New Year?" Carlos thought to himself as he reviewed the first quarter business results. It seemed like it all happened so fast with the initial actions to expand their international business. His thoughts took him back to the first quarter operations review two days ago when he and the entire senior leadership team reviewed the results across every business unit and function. In past years, this would have been a tedious exercise that would virtually shut down the business for a week in order to compile all the information necessary to see if the company was meeting its goals. He had to chuckle at how relatively painless the process was because of the work they put in at the end of last year using the Business Alignment Maturity Model©.*

A key difference between successful leaders and those who struggle is the successful leaders have a laser-like focus on desired results. Their goals are clear at all levels of the organization because they effectively communicate what they need to achieve and why those results are important to the success of the organization. They avoid the trap of letting the activity level blind them into confusing activities with results. For example, an organization's leaders might have previously looked at the number of people trained as their key people metric. Training is an activity meant to generate a desired result. The same leaders should realize training is merely an activity that is a means to achieve an end result, not the result itself. Now those same leaders look at employee engagement as part of the Balanced Scorecard process and can see more clearly how fluctuations in employee engagement levels have a direct relationship to the other areas of the business.

Having a laser-like focus on desired results takes the discussion around the results, relative to the stated goals, to a deeper level of understanding. Consciously looking at how any gaps between actual results and the predetermined goals impact the Strategy leads directly to Stage 4 Alignment. Ultimately these conversations return to the organization's Vision as the full measure of the Strategy unfolds. And as organizational leadership becomes more focused, it becomes much easier to actually "see" what success would look like and continue describing the operational intent to the rest of the organization. When everyone in the organization is tied into the alignment process, there exists a much clearer understanding of how each team's tactics impact other business unit strategies throughout the organization.

*Phil's new Strategy to expand his business to a broader audience was showing positive results. He expanded his online presence with the longer-term goal of generating more O2O (On-line to On-site) traffic. As business picked up, Phil reflected how he had recently reviewed the first quarter results with his staff. The meeting, he recalled, started slowly because it was the first time he had shared this level of detail about the business with his staff. Even though the staff had been engaged in the planning process, now they were collectively holding themselves accountable to the results of their plan.*

Achieving desired results is a function of active engagement in the process by everyone in the organization. A methodology in which leaders know in near-real time how it is performing against its goals provides the impetus and motivation to make adjustments on the move. This is more effective when people in the organization are part of the planning process, as the above example of Phil's retail business team shows. In larger organizations, such as the example of Carlos, key people from across the organization actively participate in the planning process and become part of the communications conduit for the plan.

When the organization is invested in the plan in some way or another, they execute with a sense of purpose!

However, reviewing the results against the goals is merely a first step in the process of achieving desired results. Each review must follow with a "Call to Action" to close the gaps identified. In this context, a call to action means there are specific decisions and actions identified to leverage the results for continuous improvement and continuous progress towards achieving the organization's Vision and Strategy. This is achieved through the alignment process enabling a greater understanding of the most important goals. Armed with this clarity of understanding and higher engagement level by the people in the organization as a whole, the call to action becomes a natural product of the alignment process. It is easier to create an effective call to action when the organization has a clear mental picture of what success looks like.

*Chrissy pulled into her driveway returning from a board retreat that Saturday morning. She was still reveling in how the board had worked with the staff to use the retreat to review and compare the program results with the new Strategy. She could not remember the last time they had actually done that. It was a bit awkward during the first hour as they reviewed actual Balanced Scorecard results versus the goals they created the previous quarter. During the second hour, they broke into groups, each taking a deeper look at a single goal. It was during this exercise she noticed some board members commenting on how much more clearly they understood the organization's programs based on how the goals connected to the strategy and vision.*

Achieving desired results or outcomes is critical in all organizations, both for-profit and not-for-profits. Every dollar adds to the ability of the organization to continue executing its Vision and Mission. By addressing the alignment between goals and strategy through scientific methods and metrics, organizational leaders create a continuous evolutionary process of evaluation, adjustment and success. "Success begets more

Success," as the saying goes. When organizational leaders create a culture of collaboration through effectively communicating the "picture" of success, their organizations, businesses and non-profits will achieve their desired results and Stage 4 Business Alignment.

## *QUESTIONS TO ASK:*

55.    *What does success in your business look like?*
_____
_____

     *How do you know you've achieved it?*
_____
_____

56.    *How do leaders in your organization define success?*
_____
_____

57.    *How often do you discuss business results with your organization?*
_____
_____

     *What is the structure of those conversations?*
_____
_____

58.    *Who do you share your business results with in the organization?*
_____
_____

     *Are you covering all key internal stakeholders?*
_____
_____

59.   What decisions come out of reviewing the results with internal stakeholders?

_____

_____

60.   How do your business results impact your Strategy?

_____

_____

61.   What do the results say about the People, Processes and supporting Technology currently used by the organization?

_____

_____

What adjustments or changes need to be made?

_____

_____

# A CALL TO ACTION:

"We are what we repeatedly do.
Excellence, then, is not an act but a habit."

~ Aristotle

**THE KEY POINT:** As with anything that has multiple moving parts, to the degree all the moving parts are in perfect alignment, optimal operation is the outcome. Machines, People and Organizations all require alignment on some level to achieve optimal performance. The Business Alignment Maturity Model© creates the framework to achieve optimal performance in organizations. Whether they are global businesses, local small businesses or non-profit organizations, the principles of business alignment apply to all. Due to the ever-changing business environment, the alignment process is continuous. Our journey continues to achieve Stage 5 Alignment, reached only through repetitive success through the previous four Stages of business alignment.

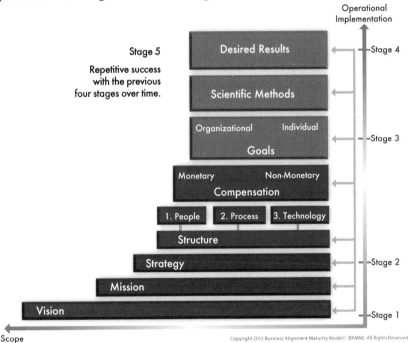

## *A Call to Action*

Achieving Stage 4 Business Alignment is not the end of the road, but rather the beginning of sustainable success. Achieving desired results under the business alignment process is similar to Dr. W. Edwards Deming's Plan-Do-Check-Act (PDCA) Cycle[1].

Machines, people and organizations must always be checked and re-checked for optimal performance. Leading an organization to the point where it achieves desired results against a stated strategy is good. Doing it repeatedly is greatness! Therefore, Stage 5 Business Alignment is creating the culture of success such that alignment occurs repeatedly!

This is the point where the journey turns to you, the Reader. As you answered the questions at the end of each chapter, you know where the alignment strengths and weaknesses are in your business and organization. You now have enough information to get started. It is up to you, the Reader, to put this information in the context of your business so you can create the solutions to achieve Stage 4, and ultimately Stage 5 Success. You may not know where to start so feel free to go to www.MissingPieceBook.com where you will find additional help in getting started. Business is a puzzle that gets more complicated as time goes on. The Business Alignment Maturity Model© is the picture on the box to help you successfully complete the puzzle and achieve Sustainable Desired Results. As a leader of, or in, a business, large or small, for-profit or not-for-profit, business alignment helps set the foundation for the strategies, goals and methodologies necessary to achieve sustainable success and help you become a lifelong leader. How will your puzzle come together?

*Lead Well!*

"The Art of Progress is to Manage Order amid Change and to Manage Change amid Order"

~ *Alfred North Whitehead*

# Endnotes

## Chapter 3

Page 34  Michael Porter[1], *Competitive Strategy: Techniques for Analyzing Industries and Competitors*, New York: The Free Press, 1980.

Page 36  Rick Page[2], *Hope is Not a Strategy*, New York: McGraw-Hill, 2002.

## Chapter 4

Page 48  Jim Collins[1], *Good to Great: Why Some Companies Make the Leap... and Others Don't*, New York: Harper Collins, 2001

## Chapter 5

Page 52  Frederick Herzberg[1], Bernard Mausner and Barbara Bloch Snyderman, *The Motivation to Work*, New Jersey: Transaction Publishers, 1993.

## Chapter 7

Page 70  Robert S. Kaplan & David P. Norton[1], *The Balanced Scorecard: Translating Strategy into Action*, Harvard College, 1996.

## A Call to Action

Page 84  Dr. W. Edwards Deming, *Out of the Crisis*, MIT Center for Advanced Engineering, 1986. [1]

## ABOUT THE AUTHOR

Rick Lochner is the President and CEO of RPC Leadership Associates, Inc. He is an accomplished Coach, Facilitator, College Professor, Keynote and Workshop Speaker, Author and foremost, a Leader.

His Vision is to help Business Owners, Corporate and Non-Profit Leadership Teams and Individual Professionals Make Leadership a Way of Life. He coaches organizational leaders to leverage effective goal-setting, organizational planning, people development and process improvement to ensure their business strategies achieve their desired results.

Rick Lochner is a graduate of the United States Military Academy at West Point and spent his 11-year military career leading soldiers in challenging environments around the globe. After leaving the Army, he spent the next 18 years in corporate leadership positions ranging from front-line management to senior executive management. He successfully led organizations in Fortune 100 corporations and privately held entrepreneurial ventures across multiple industries both for-profit and non-profit.

In addition to his undergraduate studies, Rick holds both an MS and MBA. He is a Visiting Professor at the Keller Graduate School of Management where he teaches a variety of leadership-related topics including 21st Century Leadership, Managing Organizational Change and Strategic Management.

Rick gives back to the local community as a member of the Board of Directors for Literacy DuPage, as well as the Naperville Area Chamber of Commerce Board of Directors. He and his wife, Colleen, reside in Naperville, IL.

# NOTES:

Made in the USA
Lexington, KY
21 December 2012